Christopher Columbus

A Random House PICTUREBACK®

Christopher

PIERO VENTURA

The Library of Congress cataloged the first printing of this title as follows: Ceserani, Gian Paolo. Christopher Columbus. SUMMARY: A brief biography of Christopher Columbus highlighting his ocean voyages and discovery of new lands. Translation of Il Viaggio di Colombo. 1. Colombo, Cristoforo—Juvenile literature. 2. America—Discovery and exploration—Spanish—Juvenile literature. 3. Explorers—Spain—Biography—Juvenile literature. [1. Columbus, Christopher. 2. Explorers. 3. America—Discovery and exploration] I. Ventura, Piero. II. Title. E111.C413 970.01'5'0924 [B] [92] 77-86146. ISBN: 0-394-83908-0 (B.C.); 0-394-83907-2 (trade); 0-394-93907-7 (lib. bdg.).

Manufactured in the United States of America.   A B C D E F G H I J   1 2 3 4 5 6 7 8 9 0

Columbus

Based on the text by Gian Paolo Ceserani

39678

RANDOM HOUSE NEW YORK

COLUMBUS THE GENOESE

Christopher Columbus was one of the greatest sailors and explorers of all time. He was born in Genoa, Italy, in 1451. His father was a wool weaver and, as a boy, Christopher helped him at the loom.

But Genoa was an important seaport, and Christopher dreamed of going to sea. While he was just a teenager, he left his family and joined the crew of a Genoese ship. By the time Christopher was 25 years old, he had made several voyages and had many stories to tell.

In 1477 Columbus went to live in Lisbon, Portugal. There his brother, Bartholomew, had a shop where he sold sailing charts and ship's instruments to seamen. Young Christopher met and talked to these seamen. He began to have ideas of his own about exploring.

By that time Portuguese seamen had explored the African coast. They had discovered a group of islands west of Portugal called the Azores and had set up colonies in the Madeiras, a group of five islands off the coast of Africa. They had also made voyages farther out into the Atlantic Ocean in search of new lands.

These voyages of discovery had proved that many of the old sea legends were wrong. Most seamen no longer believed the stories about horrible sea monsters or "the mysterious sea," where darkness covered everything. Scholars, navigators, and merchants were beginning to agree that the earth was round and not flat, as most people had once thought. But no one knew the real size of the world. That was still a mystery.

*The World As Columbus
Believed It To Be*

What the Portuguese wanted to do was reach the Indies. (The "Indies" at that time included India, China, the East Indies, and Japan.) At the beginning of the 14th century, another explorer, Marco Polo, had reached China by traveling east on land. He had brought back many treasures and had spoken of the great and very rich island of Cipango, or Japan. But his trip had taken a long time. The Portuguese wanted to use the sea as a faster way to get the treasures and spices. They thought they could reach the Indies by sailing around Africa. But Columbus believed that that was the hard way to get there. He was sure that sailing west would be a better plan.

However, Columbus had a difficult time selling his idea. Advisers to King John II of Portugal were sure that Columbus had made a big mistake when he guessed at the size of the world and the width of the Atlantic Ocean. King John finally refused to supply the money for the voyage, because his advisers told him the trip was impractical.

THE DEPARTURE

After many years King Ferdinand and Queen Isabella of Spain finally agreed to supply the money for his voyage. On August 3, 1492, the fleet sailed from Palos, Spain.

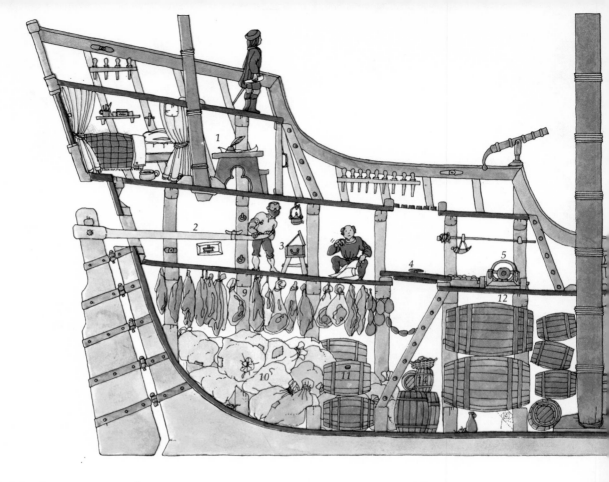

THE SANTA MARÍA, THE PINTA, AND THE NIÑA

The names of Columbus' three sailing vessels were the *Niña*, the *Pinta*, and the *Santa María*. The *Santa María* was the largest, but it was also the slowest and it was hard to sail. Although Columbus set out in the *Santa María*, his favorite ship was the little *Niña*. He made the return voyage in the *Niña* and used it for two other trips to the New World.

All three ships were very small when compared with today's ships. The *Santa María* was only about 75 to 90 feet (23 to 27 meters) long. Some modern liners are about 1,000 feet (300 meters) long.

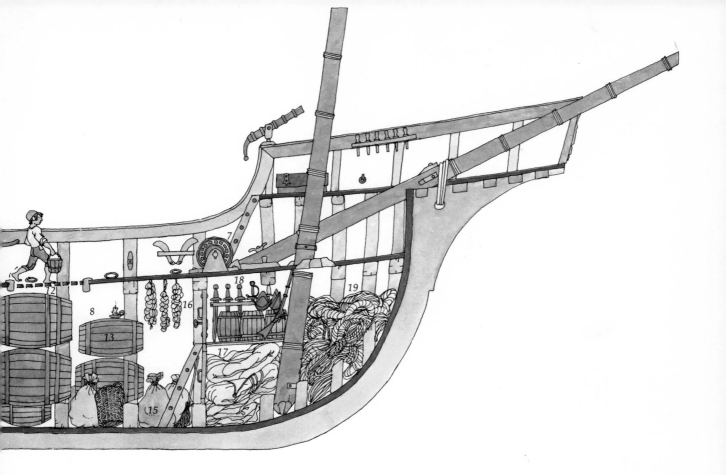

All the ships were built of wood, and they were crowded and uncomfortable. Each one had an upper deck, a quarter deck that contained the captain's cabin, and a hold, in which the cargo was placed.

Here is a cross section of the *Santa María:* (1) Columbus' cabin; (2) helm; (3) compass; (4) hatch to get down to the hold; (5) cannon; (6) pump to draw water from the hold; (7) winch for handling the sails and anchor; (8) hold; (9) salted meat; (10) biscuits and hardtack; (11) sardines and anchovies in salt water; (12) water; (13) wine; (14) oil; (15) flour and wheat; (16) garlic and onions; (17) sails; (18) arms and gunpowder; (19) ropes and hawsers.

THE CREW

There were 90 men aboard the three ships that sailed for the Indies. The *Santa María* had 40 crew members, the *Pinta* had 26, and the *Niña* 24.

There were three officials besides Columbus on the *Santa María*. The captain was the most important man on board. The second in command was directly in charge of the crew, and the pilot directed the navigation, made notes on how far they traveled every day, and decided what kind of sails to use. Not everyone on board was a sailor, however. There were also a clerk, a police officer, and two royal officials. In addition, each ship had a surgeon. Some other important people were the boatswain, who was in charge of equipment; the storekeeper, who was responsible for the supplies; a carpenter; a caulker, who repaired cracks that often appeared in the hull; and a cooper, who took care of the barrels, casks, and metal parts of the ship. The others were plain sailors who had to do the most humble jobs.

sailor   sailor   sailor   sailor   sailor   sailor

sailor   sailor   sailor   sailor   sailor   ship's boy

Columbus

captain

second in command

pilot

interpreter

police officer

clerk

royal official

royal official

boatswain

surgeon

storekeeper

carpenter

cooper

caulker

sailor

sailor

sailor

sailor

sailor

captain's boy

ship's boy

ship's boy

ship's boy

ship's boy

ship's boy

ship's boy

THE SARGASSO SEA

Though Columbus was a brave man, he was helped by good luck. He had fair trade winds and smooth seas during most of his voyage. And he managed to avoid the hurricane season by stopping for repairs and supplies in the Canary Islands. Many ships had tried to cross the Atlantic, but they had been shipwrecked or forced to turn back because of accidents. If Columbus had not discovered land, he and his men could easily have died from hunger and thirst while trying to reach the Indies. Certainly his extraordinary good fortune helped Columbus to succeed where so many others had failed.

Never was a voyage toward the unknown so calm and uneventful. One interesting thing that happened was the ships' passage through the Sargasso Sea. This area of the North Atlantic Ocean, about 2,000 miles west of the Canary Islands, is set apart from the open ocean by the mass of seaweed which floats on its surface. Early navigators had made up myths and legends about the Sargasso Sea. They thought that huge monsters of the deep lived there. Many people believed that no ship could escape once it had become entangled in the net of seaweed. But Columbus' ships proved that there was no danger in crossing the Sargasso Sea. For days and days the ships moved through the seaweed until the sailors paid no attention to it at all. Because of this, Christopher Columbus is given the credit for the first accurate report on the Sargasso Sea.

LIFE ON BOARD

The men who make up the crew of a ship live together for weeks or months. Without strict discipline and order, these men are likely to grow restless or rebellious. Because of this, all work is carried out according to rigid rules.

What was life like aboard ship in the time of Columbus? The sailors were divided into two groups or "watches." Every four hours the two groups switched. Half the crew ran the ship while the other half rested, except in case of storms or other trouble. Sleeping was difficult, however, because only a few of the officers had bunks. There wasn't even a special area for sleeping. The sailors lay down on deck, in the open, without undressing.

When the "watch" changed, orders were passed to the next watch, and a new lookout went up to the top of the highest mast. The helmsman who was going off duty shouted the ship's course to the captain. He in turn told the new helmsman, who shouted it out loud. That way there was no possibility of making a mistake. The rest of the men on duty cleaned the deck, put up the sails, and knotted the ropes. The sailmaker patched the sails, the cooper repaired barrels, and the boatswain watched over everything and passed along the captain's orders.

Food was cooked on a wood-burning stove on deck. Most meals were dry. A sailor ate biscuits and hardtack, salted meat, oil, cheese, chickpeas, honey, rice, garlic, onions, almonds, and raisins. Each ship carried flour, wheat, and some barrels of salted sardines and anchovies. The only beverages were wine and water. These foods did not have much vitamin C, which is found in fresh citrus fruits and some vegetables. So sailors often developed a terrible illness called scurvy. This produced sores and thin blood. It wasn't until 1795 that the British Navy started to give daily rations of lemon juice to its men to help prevent the disease.

A NEW WORLD

After three weeks of sailing, Columbus' crew wanted to turn back. But Columbus persuaded them to sail on.

Finally, on October 12, 1492, they sighted land—a small island in the Bahamas. Columbus landed on the beach and claimed the land for Spain. Then he knelt and gave thanks to God.

TWO PEOPLES MEET EACH OTHER

On the next day, Columbus and his men met the Arawak, the inhabitants of the island. Since Columbus believed that this island was part of the Indies, near Japan or China, he called the people he met there Indians. These people were friendly, but Columbus soon realized that they were speaking an unknown language. They did not look like the people of the Indies that other explorers had described. Also, he had been hoping to find great riches. Indeed, the purpose of the expedition was to bring back treasure and spices. Columbus was surprised to see that these people had very simple possessions. He wrote: "They . . . brought us parrots, balls of cotton thread, lances, and such trifles as they owned, and we traded small bells and other trinkets for them."

Columbus did hear the Arawak speak of another island on which there was supposed to be a great quantity of gold. As soon as the ships had taken on fresh water, they started off in search of it.

THE MOUNTAINS AND COAST OF CUBA

The island the people had talked about was Cuba. On October 28, 1492, the ships sailed into one of its bays. Columbus thought they had finally reached part of China. He explored several harbors and sent men inland to look for Peking, a Chinese city. He hoped that they could present a letter from King Ferdinand and Queen Isabella to the emperor of China. But the men found no emperor and very little gold. Columbus had to settle for the beauty of the land, which he wrote about in his journal: "The scenery and the air are the sweetest I have ever observed until now, because of the height and the beauty of the mountains."

Columbus explored the coast of Cuba with great care, looking for gold. A skillful navigator, he was not afraid to travel upstream on the rivers and push into the interior.

He visited many villages and found the huts to be simple and very clean. The islanders were all busy hunting, cooking, or building canoes.

A WORLD OF NEW PLANTS

During his exploration, Columbus often wished he had a botanist with him—someone who could study the many unknown plants they found. He wrote in his journal, "This world is the most beautiful I have ever seen, and I never get tired of looking at the splendid vegetation, so different from ours. I believe there are many plants and trees here that would be very much appreciated in Spain, but I am not familiar with them."

Columbus was right in thinking that Europeans would appreciate these new plants. Corn, potatoes, beans, tomatoes, the cacao tree, and the rubber tree were just a few of the plants he found in the New World. One plant made the Spanish especially curious. The Indians rolled up leaves from this plant and put them into a nostril. Then they lit the outer end and inhaled the smoke. It was the first time Europeans had seen tobacco!

corn

potato

beans

peanuts

papaya

cacao (cocoa) bean

pineapple

pepper

strawberry

chinaberry

tobacco

avocado

tomato

rubber tree

THE SHIPWRECK OF THE SANTA MARÍA

After exploring Cuba, Columbus sailed along the north coast of the island he named Hispaniola. On Christmas Eve, the helmsman of the *Santa María* foolishly left a ship's boy in charge of the rudder while the helmsman took a nap. Suddenly there was a tremendous crash! The ship had jammed its prow against a coral reef near Haiti. Columbus wept when he realized that the ship was lost. The local Indian chief helped save the cargo. At dawn his people helped the Spaniards carry ashore everything that could be saved. Their honesty touched Columbus. He wrote that not a single nail was stolen.

THE END OF THE FIRST VOYAGE

Columbus realized that he must now return to Spain. With one less ship he decided to build a fort and leave part of the crew in the New World.

Many of the men were glad to stay behind because they still hoped to find gold. They established the first colony in the New World. Columbus spent two more weeks looking for the Indies. But by January 16, 1493, he had not found anything like those countries. So he sailed for home on the *Niña*.

The voyage back to Spain was much more dangerous than the westward crossing had been. There were many terrible storms, and the *Niña* almost sank. But Columbus finally arrived home safely on March 15, 1493.

Columbus went to Barcelona to give Ferdinand and Isabella a report of his adventures. They gave him a grand reception and named him "Admiral of the Ocean Sea" and "Viceroy of the Indies." They asked him to arrange a second voyage, settle Hispaniola, and explore further.

Columbus did make three more voyages to America, but they were not as successful as the first. His good luck had run out, and his health failed.

Columbus died on May 20, 1506, surrounded by his two sons, one of his former captains, and a few faithful servants.